Don't Forget
the Couscous

Don't Forget the Couscous

Amir Darwish

STACK
BOOKS

Smokestack Books
1 Lake Terrace, Grewelthorpe, Ripon HG4 3BU
E-mail: info@smokestack-books.co.uk
www.smokestack-books.co.uk

ISBN 978-0-9931490-3-0

Smokestack Books is represented
By Inpress Ltd

‘

To lovers everywhere,
particularly the Kurds
among them as they wonder
landless around the globe.

'A *poet's work is to name the unnameable,*
to point at frauds, to take sides, start arguments,
shape the world and stop it from going to sleep.'
Salman Rushdie

Contents

Sorry!

*An apology from Muslims (or those perceived to be Muslims)
to humanity*

We are sorry for everything
That we have caused humanity to suffer from.
Sorry for Algebra and the letter X.
Sorry for all the words we throw at you;
Amber, candy, chemistry, cotton, giraffe, hazard,
Jar, jasmine, jumper, lemon, lime, lilac,
Oranges, sofa, scarlet, spinach,
Talisman, tangerine, tariff, traffic, tulips,
Mattress (yes mattress) and the massage you enjoy on it:
We are sorry for all of these.

Sorry that we replaced alcohol with coffee for Enlightenment
    philosophers.
Speaking of hot drinks,
We are sorry for the cappuccino the Turks brought over.
Sorry for the black Arabian race horses,
For the clock,
Maths,
Parachutes.

Abdul in the US is sorry for what so and so did;
He does not know him but he is sorry anyway.
Sorry that we accompanied Columbus on his journey to the States.
And sorry for the Arab man with him
Who was the first to touch the shore and shout 'Honolulu'
And named the place after him.
Sorry for the architecture in Spain and the Al Hambra palace there.
We apologise for churches in Seville
With their stars of David at the top that we built with our hands.
We say sorry for every number you use in your daily life from the 0 to
    the trillion.
Even Adnan the Yezidi (mistaken for a Muslim)
Is sorry for the actions of Abu whatever who beheads people in Syria.

Sorry for the mercury chloride that heals wounds,
Please give us some –
Because the guilt of initiating all of the above
Gives us a wound as big as this earth.
Sorry for the guitar that was played by Moriscos in Spain
To ease their pain when they were kicked out of their homes.
Sorry for the hookah as you sip on its lips
And gaze into the moon hearing the Arabian Nay.
Sorry for cryptanalysis and the ability to analyse information systems,
To think what is at the heart of the heart of the heart and bring it to
    the world.
Sorry for painting Grenada white to evade social hierarchy.
Sorry for the stories in *The Arabian Nights*.

Every time we see a star, we remember to be sorry for Astronomy.
We are sorry that Mo Farah claimed asylum here
And went to become the British champion of the world.
Sorry for non-representational art,
Pattern and surface decoration.
We are sorry for all the food we brought over:
From tuna to chicken tikka masala,
Hummus,
Falafel,
Apricot,
Doner kebab
Right up to the *shawarma* roll.
And don't forget the couscous.

If we forgot to apologise for something, never mind,
We are sorry for it without even knowing it.
Most of all we are sorry for Rumi's love poems,
And we desperately echo one of them to you:

Oh Beloved,
Take me.
Liberate my soul.
Fill me with your love and
Release me from the two worlds.
If I set my heart on anything but you
Let fire burn me from inside.

Oh Beloved,
Take away what I want.
Take away what I do.
Take away what I need.
Take away everything
That takes me from you.

Please forgive us.
We are sorry and cannot be sorry enough today.

I am

I am a chicken tikka masala in a Sunday night take-away for lovers.
I am Mohammed to my Parisian friends but Jacques on my CV.
I am a Friday night *doner kebab* after a good night out.
I am a taxi driver ready to pick up and drop you on a cold winter day.
I am a doctor, a white angel whose touch will make it better.
I am a London *sheesha* smelling of apple.
I am an off-license shop with a pint of milk ready for tea when guests
   arrive.
I am hot-to-touch *naan* bread.
I am a little boy who cannot understand why my school-friends won't
   play with me anymore.
I am a New York pizza delivery boy who is spat at when I deliver food.
I am a young girl who has taken off the *hijab* in order to feel safe.
I am an old man who has started to shave my beard.
I am a grandmother who has exchanged the *zari* for a pair of jeans.
I am a mosque with broken windows.
I am a Muslim.
I am not a terrorist.

I feel I should speak of the city

I feel like I should speak of the city;
Of its roads, alleys, streets and shops
Assembled in line with their bumpy stoned paths
Striking reflexology pulses into feet;
Of the castle that never sleeps
Keeping lovers near it, tattooed to its heels;
Of coffee shops that strike laughter into ears on each card played,
Each tea glass Din Din on the table
And each ringing phone as heads turn towards passing beauties;
It is the city where sellers of cakes roll their chariots
And shout, *'move before I strike your belly'*;
Of the barbers who roll strings on fingers
Threading pulling and pushing back and forth unplucking hairs
As they wave to passers *Assalamu Alaikum*;
Of the children on Eid and their colourful clothing;
Toy pistol guns; polished shoes;
Tiny fingers as they kiss the hand of the elders and run to feast.
And the Arabian sweets, and *kanafeh*, and *kobbah*,
And vine leaves and *shawarma* combined with hummus
Melting into the hands of taxi drivers as they swing their *Tasbih*
and say حلـو يـا رايـح ويـن ;
The veg sellers and mountains of tomatoes, mandarins, apples
And the red blood-like halved figs next to dangling bananas;
Of the smoothie-sellers with their non-stop mixers,
And their boys collecting money,
Flipping 25 Syrian lira in the air and catching it in their pockets.

Yes, it is the city and its trees,
The leaves, the roundabouts in it
And the smell of petrol
As they mix with hot summer burning Middle Eastern sun.
The beauty of girls as they speak, catwalk,
Adjust their *yashmaks*, remove their anklets,
Smell their lovers' handkerchiefs,
Cry as they nudge one another sheepishly
And point out cute boys they are promised to.

It is the shining marble at *Le Meridian* hotel
That has stripes of gold reflecting the giant chandelier above
As I move my head back and forth it gets closer and further from me.
The narrative of mothers, lecturing fathers,
The cruelty of brothers, loving sisters, emotional lecturers
All as they gather around giant Ramadan banquets
Of lentil soup as it strikes hot smoke
Into the eyes of those who love it most
And blow air into spoonfuls of hot boiled sage before giving it to
  babies.

And the long queues in Aleppo central park
For weekenders to buy boiled corns, spray them salt,
Take the first bite and spit it out, '*oh it's too hot*'.

Of the ticketing offices and their touch me not secretaries
Who head hunt tourists from their dark, brown, smooth, firm office
  desks;
Of each corner, each turn, each give and take haggling in bazaars
And each wool seller in the medina
As he mixes red with green over blue on white
To attract the veiled eyes of his lover;
And of old men and their wrinkled hands as they place one over
  another,
Close their eyes and pray at Zakrya Mosque
Loosing themselves in spirituality.

I speak of Aleppo City.

Syrian belly dancer

to Basher al-Assad

UN. Fountain of blood. Ready.
The stage is set for you.
You appear
Men clap
Hips examined, re-examined again and again.

Belly-dancing costume not too revealing!
They shout.
You take off a layer
Then another and another,
Not yet nude, but you will be soon.

Up you jump, landing in the fountain of blood.
SPLASH!
You splash the watching men,
Their tongues slide out, roaming over aces licking blood,
Unreachable spots lickable by others next to them.

They enjoy it.
'Do it again, again,' they chant.

Up you jump, landing more firmly.
SPLASH!
Blood flies, reaching glasses, faces, food.
Glasses are emptied, food is eaten, faces are licked.
Loud clapping.

Jump, land, splash
Jump, land, splash
Jump, land, splash
There is no more blood left in the fountain.
But they still ask for more.

The statue of Liberty on Syria

Veinless, bloodless, eyes glued eastwards,
Knee half-bent ready for the first step,
Belly-button deep, and swallow barbarism;
Hips curvy, mouth silently loud, earlessly hearing
Long haired, voyage, lineless balms, steady foot
An olive nose, scent of liberty, breathes in, exhales,
Sending a breeze across Syrian beaches, fetching
Human fragments across the globe, humanising
Statues, a great choice says the statue of liberty:

'No better nation can de-statue us
Bring me the bravery of the Arab Knights
Plant in me Arab literature
Let its branches flower in my body.
Gather me sunflower seeds, or those
Blossom roses, walnuts from Efrin that
Resemble brains when crushed, lay
Before me lemons, that strike gas into
The tearful eye ball when squeezed,
Kill no time, congregate stones of
Ancient civilizations; those who only
Speak the language of statues:
Mother Russia, Christ the Redeemer and David.
Proliferate our race, Florence awaits,
Today is the day to declare our
Superiority, Long live the progeny of statues.'

You, who thought the world could change

You, who thought the world could change –
Don't be disappointed
Drop a stone in the pool of your lover's eyes,
Watch its water flood
Its tsunami
Drown the sweet land of liberty.

You who never find pleasure in things
Consider a lover who walks on your back barefoot,
Leaving scars as she marches.
Find a corner in yourself
Stay put
Quiet,
Faceless in the middle of an eye
Let your fingers crush red-hot charcoals: then swallow them.

Each moment
Each place
Each nothingness
Use them to walk on
As dusk fall into night
Then into cities
And lastly to your eyes.

We have just arrived at the entrance of Arabia

We are at the entrance of Arabia
Where smells of spices walk in our heads
Lose themselves in our brains' streets
And dissolve into crowd of notions
As we blink to one another in agreement.

Suddenly
The world vanishes into our shimmering eyes
Where reflections show men of steel falling into
Lines of honour
We stare lengthy into each other.

My *habiby*
It's dawn at the gates of our hearts
So
Let sit
Break the fast
By the bank of our arteries.

We need hairless, seedless skins
To empty our sentimental tongues and
Water love to watch it grow
Old
Strong
Wise
Mature
Then see it fade into our souls forever.

Sweetheart
Let's halt ships of honour
When they depart the flood of tears,
Then let them loose into
The pool of your eyes.

Let see how much you can take into your
Fun-loving
Carefully crafted shrine
As we both truthfully speak nonsense
Fall out of reality
And into love again and again.

There must be a light at the end of this tunnel

There must be a light at the end of this tunnel
At a point where
So many eyes look into darkness
Cut through a bone and
Shine it.

There will be a creature there
A strange one
With no hands
No lips
No arms
No ears
No body
And only eyes
Eyes and soul.

That being will find a light from within you
And strike it out to the world.

Over there
In that place
The river of sadness dries
Melancholy waves hush and
The Sorrow garden
Reflects an Arabian desert moonlight
Shining the universe.

There
You sit with your hand back and forth
Playing the water of a Damascus fountain.

The world

Is a stone.
A child in a Baghdad street kicks it
And a drop of water
Cultivates all the deserts of Dubai so it can flower.

It is an eye-ball reflecting the sun
Then blinking to swallow the earth.

Or maybe it is a vase
Near a window
In Aleppo.

As I stare at it,
My vision expands, wide as the river Nile.

Today, it feels best to write about this relationship

Today,
It feels best to write about this body and soul relationship.
Write for example:
The exchange of gifts when your kidneys throb with pain
But you stay on the dance floor.
The eyes are two sockets with straight sharp unbroken light
From Aleppo all the way to the moon.
This entire body is like a sea
Deep
Blue
Wavy
Huge
Beautiful and
Devoted to its watchers.
Or maybe it's a red square with snow fur and thick with mud
Like a milk chocolate skin

The lips are two still ships
That only move millimetres when seen from the shore.

Lashes no longer protective
Lean towards each other and in love forever
The two eyebrows above them are two feathers from the 12th century
Light they are,
Yet heavy with words.

A plea to a lover not to leave

Like a snake, skin me off your body
      Or peel me like an onion in a Kurdish woman's hand

With a sharp tweezers, hair by hair unpluck me off yourself

      I fear this desert in your eye soon will storm me blind

    The eyebrows above it
Like an Arabian sword
Cut me delicately and my blood seeps for you

I left you lilies last autumn
Now you are a thorn
Pointed
Ready to stab

What
If
Why
How
Where
When
Are all not you
Nothing like you

    Our love story is so long
It will last to judgment day
Let us say the body is a lake
Deeeeeeeeeeeeeep I dive in it
    Or maybe it is a lilac
I walk its leaves barefoot
Naked
Fearless like a 9th century Arabian Caliph

I find pleasure nowhere my love but here in your navel, eat
Drink
Smoke
Walk
Talk
Draw and live here

Vertigo as my eyes touch you walk on their lids

As statue of tears sculpts itself in my eyeball and is about to blow itself up

Beautiful home of mine
Stay in my veins
Dry them like a pomegranate branch falling dead in the middle of a
Syrian August
Then hold it up and break it in halves
Sweet, sweet sultana you melt in my mouth

Like a remnant of your favourite meal I stay between your teeth
Refuse to come out
I push myself in as you move your tongue over me

The dusk has gone to sleep in your hair and I am its loyal guard

I sit with my eyes wide open to watch you fall cell by cell into me
Then I collect you and leave

It is too late in the night to speak of departure
Look out the widow
Look
The moon is here
Dancing on your skin
The stars landing on your lashes like glitter now you shine from a
distance
I smeared myself in your blood
Now you want to cleanse me

Like Adam and Eve were the first two
We are the last two
Don't go
Or else
There will be no more lovers left.

Like a River

Like a river that went on strike
Last millennium you are
Frozen
Unmoved
Unknown

In a land of lovers you walk
Between passion trees
Your head nudges the fruit
So they fall

The stream near you
Is the line to ecstasy

Here is the heart
Use it as a boat
Sail
Stretch your hand
Pluck roses from the Garden of Eden

At your side
An Arabian gazelle walks with you
Dawn opens the sky
And you reach the gate.

Welcome home sweetheart.

Imprisoned Tongues

They imprisoned our tongues
And declared our sex speechless

Like two Babylonian stones
Our eyes are now useless.

Palestine

Palestine is a rose that rose
To refresh the air as it enters the nose.

It's all about love

Be grateful for everything written about love
From the first ink humanity slaughtered in Syria
To this very last exact word right now on this page: LOVE.

Love is a *misbaha*:
Full of beads
Suddenly
Cut loose on the world
To drown lovers up to their ears
Leaving only the brain
To think of love.

Love like a red wall in the Al Hambra
Blushes when you enter.

It is an Andalusian *hammam*
A scar left for ever on the face of Granada.

Love is a palm tree in Fes
Taaaalllllll with a nest at its top
Grass on grass assembled by lovebirds.

Love is a poem you perfect for months
And like an ardent and sexually demanding young lover
Always wants more of you.

So follow the fine line of the curve
Then rest your head in deep sleep.

Love is a tear
About to explode
In the middle of an eye.

It's a *Barkouk* with wrinkles.
The squeeze let its remnants come out of the fist
The way runny butter does.

Love rises with every virgin who keeps herself intact only for one.

Love is a pair of naked lovers in a pickle jar
Twisted on one another and promising to stay this way forever.

And this life must go on to have more of love
Be in and out of it,
Fall for it,
Around it,
Because of it.

Finally
One refuses to call love it
Or he,
Or she,
Or they,
We,
Us,
Them,
Love is different.
It is a ferry crossing between lovers' eyes.
It's in trees,
Water,
Sky,
Rivers.

It's an ember as lovers embrace
By a fire in the Atlas mountains.

And as the story goes in *The Arabian Nights*:
Love becomes a red rose that jumps into the Nazareth palace
And gives it colour
While lovers sent to the moon kissing
Stay there forever.

Love gives itself to everyone
Everywhere,
But since Eve's arrival
What it gave so far nothing but this:.................

Love is a religion
So follow its scripture
Make love at certain times a day
On Friday,
Saturday,
Or Sunday,
Or even make your own new holy day and call it:
Loveday.

Love is a wave between Tangier and the sweetheart's eyes
Daily it sails between the two.

Or maybe love is a stream of milk between a nipple
And the world to feed it tranquillity.

Love has one flavour
One colour
And no country.
Its inhabitants are everything that moves
Including this pen as it writes.

It's even in the sand clock that appears in a pupil,
Dropping endlessly as you watch it nonstop.

Love is the three quarters of the earth
Which is water,
You swallow it all
And your stomach can contain more if that is what love wants.

Love is a high mountain shadow
It appears and disappears on your lover's back nightly
As he rises up and down in the act of making love.

Love is pure and never mixes itself with hate,
Yet it is part of it
The way an oil-slick moves in the sea.

Love is beautiful

So beautiful
That when you see it
You fall into a love-coma.

Love is the best form of government that political philosophy can offer
Where you have no duty but one:
To make love.

Soukaina's eyes

The right eye consists of two oceans:
Black and white.

The white one has no land whatsoever,
                    It's all water.

The black one has an island
                    In the middle
There is a house with an Andalusian mosaic,
                    Garden
                    And gazelles
The kind that are only found in Soukaina's eyes.

Water from the white ocean often leaks,
Enters the house to wash it,
Fill the fountain in the eyeball
For gazelles to drink.

As for the left eye, there is nothing yet,
So wait and time will tell.

The Wedding Night

The skin is a soft fresh Greek yoghurt.
Dip your finger in,
Suck it,
As she encases herself under the quilt.

Shivers of adrenaline from guts
Rush blood to the heart.

For it to beat
A Middle Eastern drum on a wedding night.

Deafening one thousand attendees.
But who is complaining?

A man at Dubai Airport

At Dubai airport,
There is a man with a white bandaged broken arm.

He stops to wave.

One of his fingers has a scar.
His feet perfectly fit his Arabian slippers.

There are holes in his wrinkle free immaculate white top.
His light blue jeans are reflected in the shiny marble he stands on.
The stripes in the ten-metre high glass window behind him are grey
Like his eyes.

The sounds of planes vibrate inside his skull.

With two hands, he covers his ears
And skilfully takes off and lands the planes with his eyes.

I remember a road once

I remember a road once
So clean and neat
Straight
And planted with trees
Houses on both sides
And red cars too
Sky, moon, stars and sun
Everything was there
Everything but you.

The Jewish Cemetery in Chisinau, Moldova

It's cold.
Hands bury themselves in winter coats.
Ears ask the shoulders to rise higher.

Heavy the body from excessive wear
Moving around photographic gravestones.

They are scattered everywhere
Like cumin and red chilli on hummus.

The small alleys are identical in measurement,
Like the space between the eyebrows in one of the portraits.

Leaves heavy with snow,
Frozen
And with a delicate touch they drop on faces.

Humming birds,
Lonely wondering cats,
Street dogs
And beggars are all here for dinner.

The sun disappears beyond the biggest grave to the left.

At the exit,
The iron door has small holes,
A child tiptoes,
Squeezes an eye in one of them to watch his father's burial.

The secret spot in Budapest

Remember the spot I showed you?
It's as high as your proud forehead,
A proud moment,
Full of trees,
Clouds,
Cool breeze,
Shiny marbles
And beautiful people.

Tranquillity
Born there,
Raised glance after glance
By lovers,
Nurtured,
Then pushed off the hill
And sprinkled all over Budapest.

We held hands there.
Our fingers like an Arabian netted *yashmak*.
The wind took us slowly into
Each other's bodies.

Foreheads one on another.
We exhaled the air of love from within,
Deep we were in each other's skins.

Our arteries formed
A silk crossroad.
We were fine that way
And never was the world as perfect as at that moment.

A description of a Queen in Budapest

Dozens of birds cover her eyes in a shape of a gazelle
And lashes are swords to cut flesh
As the world hides itself in her breast.

She holds Danube-stained curative feathers,
While her marrow is full of suckable honey.

Dressed in vine leaves,
Her words are thorns plunged into ears.
Her letters are olive-oiled to smooth her commands.

Hungarian mountain rise from her ears and so does
God, Lord, Allah, or whatever you want to call it.
Budapest shakes herself loose of her body.

A waterfall of men pour from her eyes
And I am one of them.

Her mouth is a red hot wine pool,
Humanity and the Danube sink in it at once.

Then she swallows the chain bridge as a
Black Arabian horse runs the course of her hair.

She is the essence of love,
Right in the middle of a heart shape island,
Breathing fire,
Spitting hearths,
Throwing coins

That land violently in the pool of my blood.

A tree in Budapest

An Andalusian tree
Enshrines itself on
The bank of the Danube
While Budapest like a
Liver swells with hot wine.

Its soil begs for seeds
A cloud gives it drops of life.

All of Budapest
Sees it through the eye of a needle.

It will flower,
Give birth to new roads
And flash lights in the face of
Darkness
To light a love path.

The tree grows
With wrinkles as young
As the moment you read this poem.

Lovers stand near it to knit
Thoughts as beautiful as Scottish Kashmiri jumper.

Now it is an Andalusian gazelle
That leaps and leaps between
The Danube and Euphrates
Until the dry sweat creases the skin.

In a Babylonian garden
It showers
And washes away pieces of skin;
Hair,
Eye socket,
Nails,
Sins
All fall into the Euphrates
and give it colour.

This is Amsterdam

An orange hangs from a toddler's hand
As he chases pigeons near Rembrandt's statue.
One after another the buildings with colourful windows,
Inner lights and a see-through wine glass in one of them,
The sun's reflection on cutlery,
Resting upon an unwrinkled white cloth on a formica table.
The pregnant woman walking a dog that sprints
To hasten the arrival of her baby.
The flood of bicycles, ching-ching;
Girls and boys navigate through waves of humans,
They spread like millions of white pilgrims in Mecca at *Eid*.
The cyclist lights a joint while he peddles,
Enlarges his lungs with hash then disappears beyond the smoke at
    Dam Square.
The roundy cheese on display at shops
Goes darker and lighter as window shoppers pass by,
Some slow, some fast, casting their shadows over it.
And the wok that feeds thousands at Wok to Walk;
Smooth, thick with oil, big,
Proud as everyone watches, waiting and begging it for mercy and food.
The pins that hold small tiny maps at Anne Frank house,
Like the maze of a man's face scarred from childhood.
The girl with short black skirt, glass and fag in hand,
Next to the suave Dutchman who is dying to have her;
She stands one step higher than him, waves pigeons away with a leg,
He imitates her, and fakes a fall to see what's up her skirt.
The packed window with small cans of hashish plant.
The prostitute in the next window,
Twisting and turning as her red string pulls passers-by towards it,
Keeping their moral heads straight and socially in order.
The cafe with its small interior lounge,
And wooden exterior tables engraved with small lines of ash.
The small jars of salt and paper on each table,
Like a couple in love, explicitly hug each other,
The flower vase with its long thin curvy eye-catching body

Like a woman I saw in Istanbul back in 2006.
Wine glasses sit upside down, rattling to Tchaikovsky's *Nutcracker Suite*.
The nearby pub full of colourful people who finish their drinks, walk
    the moon home
And disappear beyond tiny bridges
That curve up while their arches allow fish, birds, boats, people, water
To go through neatly like an Indian string going into a needle eye
    without hitting the edges.
The canals are a poet's nerve system, constantly flushing themselves
    into cleanliness.
The mixture of smells that comes off them:
Incense, perfume, wet soil and oil as they smash their way into your
    head.
The drunken man who stands right at the edge of the bank,
Freeing a thought as wide as the Mediterranean or as narrow as his
    zigzag urine line.
The half-shy sun who plays now-you-see-me-now-you-don't
As windmills move their hands to shadow the French pearl face
Of a girl sunbathing outside Zaans' cafe.
The half-curved mini tree near her
Leaves the sun captive in its leaves
As tourists adjust their tables and chairs to escape the sunlight.
The step-by-step directions given by an eighteen year-old American
To Middle Eastern tourists who are lost, lonely and looking for
    Freedom Square.
The happy, easy-going drugged-up guy with half-fastened denim
    jacket,
Who leans towards me, 'brother, you want some coca?'

The central rail station where pigeons and stones share the same colour,
Travellers sit over their mountains of luggage,
Stare into one another, yawn and wait for the screen to flip.

The man in a suit on Platform 4 with a walkie-talkie,
While hands on lower back stretching it to point his… (you know what)
The small windows above his head with millions of holes like a Persian
   princess' dress.
The people running to catch the train, some heavy with flowers;
As they jog, tulips fall, right, left and centre like soldiers dying for the
   love of their country.

The Moroccan couple by the corner chew a Dutch pancake
And slowly gaze into emptiness.
Ducks, crows and birds nearby are fighting over the debris of bread.

Amsterdam's canals

We sit near the canal
On the right hand side of the river;
We have all the roses
Of Amsterdam.

The sky resurrects their thorns
Then turns them into rain,
They settle in our skin.

The branches grow fast.
Twice a day we jump into the canal
To water them.

A visit to Rio's Parque Lage

At the entrance the humming voices of birds
Fall like grains of sand from a fist
Full of honey, as we walk in the direction of heaven.

The fountain waters dance on love-stained stones.

The grass is in a coma beneath our feet.

At the café
Breakfast arrives
Consisting of three strokes,
Two kisses,
One spreadable gaze
And the blackness of eyes overcoming the colour of coffee.

Nonetheless, it is still raining stones in the wine-pool of your eyes,
You chew a mouthful of Copacabana sand
Then lose yourself.
Unprotected against tropical diseases, you catch one: it's called love.

Your hair is fashioned like a banana boat
That you ride to your mouth,
The lips are neither a shrine nor a meditation
But a place where ideas are slaughtered.
Your eyes are windows of hope,
White as sperm,
Wide as the Brazilian coastal line.

Suddenly,
You become a pearl in a hand,
The left eye examines you
As the right one is shut.

Near the exit, Damascus jasmines deliberately land on nipples,
Two of them,
Smell violently of love
Like a newly wedded couple in an Ottoman bed.

Rio's Cathedral

From the ceiling divinity like a sharp needle dangles into our eyes:
We accept it willingly.

What if

We were a handful of sand
Picked by Christ the Redeemer and sprinkled over Rio like rain.
We landed headfirst, hands, body and lastly our hearts.

Love's dew wet us,
We slid on leaves to become drops of purified tropical juices,
Dangled and swung while thirsty lovers below waited to receive us.

My eyes do not watch you anymore

My eyes do not watch you anymore: they touch you.
It is 3am. Rio has gone to sleep while you dawn on me.
No one is awake apart from me, you and our eyes, my dear.

As you say goodbye

As you say goodbye,
Naked eyes undress you

Facial expressions are mosaic pieces on a forehead.
Upon a kiss you giggle and blush.

Tears are sacrificed on your breast,
Drop by drop you sink into sadness.

Your hair is a tsunami, it swallows me, then dribbles
Me naked, lifeless, lonely to dance on your skin.

Like a Japanese earthquake-specific building
Your body rattles in bed and refuse to collapse.

Your lips take the shape of two crescent moons in love,
As they smile they expand, so does my thought.

Your eyebrows are an Amazonian maze,
Thousands of men could lose themselves there.

Your fingers are ten candles burning over my head
Dripping wax drop by drop to burn my eyes and quench my tears.

Flying

Sky and sea, blue is the colour above and below
We fly to a land we don't know.

In Siberia once we wrote our
Memories, now they are melted snow.

The Atlantic Ocean appears in a shape of a whale,
Meaningful glances enter our eyes

The world knows enough,
But you and I, sweetheart, we know nothing.

To write for and to Morocco

For the cities inside you Morocco,
Just like every human with a heart, each has a Medina,
The *barkouk* there, when it strikes the mouth
Sour, sweet, chewy as a tongue that bites itself by mistake.

For the Middle East, that is like a stone in a rosary,

To these letters and the ocean of ink that supply them,
The L's and O's and V's and E's, their speedy impact,
But slow encapsulation in the brain before they crush the page.

For the clock hand that constantly tries to reach someone but fails.

For the *Jemma* prayer at Hasan II mosque in Casablanca,
Where the faithful gaze at the marbles there,
Their steps as they walk inside, humble, head high ready for *Jinnah*.

To the converts among them who stroll and repeat,
'Clean at last, clean last, thank you Allah, we are clean at last';
Their eyes, mirror-like, reflect a rare mosaic
Spreading from Damascus aaaaaaaaall the way to Casablanca,

To the moon that hides itself behind the minaret,
Shy, sure of its beauty, humbly shining over worshippers.

For the love of this world and the ability to say more than few
words and be just fine.

For the wonderful world of children,
The innocent blank white sheet brain that contains only
Twinkle Twinkle Little Stars and pictures of the Muffin Man.

For the lovers I watch
As one of them cracks her lover's head open,
Fashioning an ocean of lilies in which to drown herself.

For the muscle that twitches and wobbles every split second
(To confirm its presence)
Like a Middle Eastern freshly made jelly on New Year's Eve.

For the sky that gets close to the head and the earth that pushes
　　towards it.

For these fingers as they tap on walls
While standing in dismay to decrease my...
As eyes grow wider on round backsides.

To a Marrakech desert night
Where the moon is so full your eyes have no room left to see anything
　　else.

For the filthy poetry that some walk away from and others walk
　　towards and inside.

For a previous lover on the other side of the world
And her thighs that took me in perfectly,
Her touch and gaze, her sweet, sweet tongue, gentle hands and fine
　　choice of perfume,
But most of all for the lily she placed between her breast then asked
　　me to remove it with
'My most beautiful part'.

For you when you read this poem
And let the chemicals in your brain reach the surface
Like a Moroccan tea poured so as to leave bubbles that pop, pop, pop
Before touching the dirty bottom and settle.

For the entire dirt of humanity when it leaves the kidneys,
Settles in the bladder then pushes itself out into the real world.

For the friends and friends' friends,
Those who gaze into the heart to shrink it
As a sponge sucks sadness then expands it with happiness.
For the heavily pregnant brain and the fallacy in the cleavage
That defeats the latest school of thought.

To the walls of magnificent Fes,

For the man fast asleep in an Arabian Souk,
With his wrinkles deepen with wisdom to hide the whole of Morocco
    inside them,

To the small cuts in his fingers, old and new and the stories they hold.

For the head of the tourist that fixes itself to gaze at the colourful ceiling
Of Al Bahia Palace, stares too long, then cricks its neck right and left to
    look up again.

For the chatter of sellers in Arabian medinas, drilling holes in ears,
Then hanging blue charms in them for protection from evil.

For the eye in one of these charms,
Turning itself into a battle ground where the entire world is an army
And one soldier is the eyeball, surrounded, weak, disarmed and in love.
This is the same eye that every morning turns itself into a lively Medina,
Heaves with spices for tourists to dip themselves in
And get ready for a roasting under the Arabian sun.

To the beautiful image of the hate of the world as a pinch of salt on a
    palm,
That you can blow clean.

To the beauty who places a rose in her teeth and walk her lover's bed,
Catlike towards him.

To the poet who searches for an analogy as good as two stars on the
anklet
That encircles a Middle Eastern bride;
As she walks so does the earth and the sound of her heels is meditative.

To the blood when it freezes in veins and gets heavy, as I defrost in the
Sahara.

And for the mixing of humming birds, baby cries and calls to Morning
Prayer
In a Fes Riad when it wakes me up from a sweet, sweet dream, and calls
itself Morocco.

Moroccan Heart

At a Moroccan gate
A heart of stone
Rolls off the Atlantic
Picks pitfalls on the way
Then bounces towards Marrakech.

The scream echoes in Casablanca
Near our lilac bed
Rose gardens
Ready for us to pluck.

A while ago

A while ago, group of human organs were born: a while gone
And they still sit at night gazing at the moon and counting the
    stars around them.

Dawns arrive and depart quietly, other animals indulge them
While stones bounce in and out of water until their colours fade.
The sky is blue and so are the bones.

These organs are figures gathered disorderly on the page,
Like Aleppo apples they drop from love trees: before the soil
They meet, greet, love, laugh, cry, then fall on a Syrian allotment.

Or maybe they are drops of sweat falling from a forehead,
Dispersing like pomegranate seeds in a Mediterranean land to
Grow,
Flower,
Open,
Then shoot up their blood-like red seeds into the sky.

The stream of love

There is a field
With half-metre tall tulips;
A stripy tiger sits there with his tail switching right and left;
He peers as children tiptoe their way behind him.

In the orchard
Leaves fall into love's stream.

As the spring of love begins
Trapped thoughts smuggle
Themselves into the stream
To flow, flow, flow until they are no more.

Messages, words, memories,
Everything flushes out
Of the world and
Into the stream of love.

Thoughts are like plants

Thoughts are like plants.
Like touch-me-not-lady
They close when you feel them.

Others are medicinal, healing,
Divine, meaningful, heart-flattering
As they flower inside you.

Upon a touch,
A few sting your hands with their smell.

Some will even replace their veins
With yours and your blood with dew.

Roses, lilies, tulips and jasmines
Like organs
Shiver debris of adrenaline.

Accept replacement dear friend,
Now it is fashionable to be a plant.
But as for tomorrow, you never know.

On board with feathers

Along with leaves,
Thorns and roses,
Feathers reach the sky then rain down on lovers everywhere.

They break in two and fall on Noah's Ark:
Their weight is just right.

As they sail, the waves reach up to swallow the clouds.

While I am on deck,
I crack open a sunflower seed,
And here comes an idea,
Wet as the Euphrates,
Dry as this (….) In the middle of the sea.

He is really happy

He is over the moon, happy as chains
Melting into tomorrow's dream.

Like grains of sadness
Endlessly drop from his fist.

The smile is a pregnant cloud,
Twin expected: life and happiness.

Last night's poem

I spent last night perfecting a poem
To the point where all its letters fell off the page.

Accidently my eye fell out in the process,
Ever since I have been looking everywhere for my eye.

I found all the letters, but my eye is nowhere to be seen.
Anyway, here is the poem:...................................

Imagine

Imagine that love is a river flowing
From your eyes and into lovers' hearts everywhere,

Or that my body is an African field that you
Embrace like a flock of immigrant birds.

Imagine the sunrise in your pupils
That sets beyond a pyramid of my bones,

Statues of you carved in sand,
Broken into a million pieces and re-carved again,

Imagine your heels dancing on my back
To release passion's fountain,

Or your womb exploding into
A universe full of lovers.

Him in the distance

Him in the distance
Rests in peace
Eyes gaze upwards,
Face like a full moon,
Shy of departure
In a clear summer Mediterranean sky.

He loses his body in an
Andalusian garden,
Falls on the grass
And dew invades his back
As flowers shiver
Debris on the forehead.

Nearby
The immortal fountain kills his thirst.

Yesterday, my lover sent me a message

Yesterday, my lover sent me a message:

'There is not a time
That I write to you without writing
Myself all over the page.
I never breathe
Differently as the pen
Strikes 'I' in every line
(Tell me, do I sometimes jump on you from the page?)
My dearest
Take my heart
Take it
Since it's you
Who owns it.
Nurture it as you go along
Because it no longer beats in order,
Lecture it delicately
Bring its passion down
The finest moment my darling is when
My heart halves itself: half mine, half yours.'

An Australian night

It's all happening tonight.
Fat
Thick
Drops of sperm
Fall on the page
To impregnate an entire book.

The sky bleeds stars,
Sharply lit,
The marching clouds salute.

The sea silently dries its tears
As it pours water into our sight.

Between two breasts
Hangs a tropical hammock,
Your nipples are nails.

We swing
Then jump into your belly button
Sinking deep
To leave a seed.

A fruit later emerges down under.

The holiness of her eyes

Her naked eyes
Are made of two oceans,
Black and white.

We hold them deep
In oceans beneath
The earth.

Plants grow and die unseen
Water passes from
Her eyes
To rivers
Seas
Lakes.

We hold her eyes
In an unknown place
And wherever we go
They show us the path.

We hold them
To hold what is holy to us all today,
Her beautiful eyes.
Amen.

Beauty in the Atlas Mountains

A tree
A tent
A forest
An entire Atlas inside your eye.

In the eyeball
There is fire
Naked you dance
In the middle of it.

Love birds breed in your navel
Humming the rhythm of your heart
Moths dive and die
In the pool of your liver
Full of wine.

A pine tree plants itself in your heart
We sit under its shadow, lovers as we are.

The brain

Sometimes it chews itself
Into a walnut or a fig
Full of seeds when halved

Other times
It's a poet searching for a word
Sharp as an Arabian sword.

When we die

When we die,
Will we be in a place where leaves fall in the streets
And passers-by kick them while whistling *Swan Lake*?

Will computer screens freeze
And Niagara Falls cascade into our living rooms?

When we die,
Will the clock hands halt crowds in London,
Make them immediately close their eyes,
Breathe in,
Sigh with relief
And walk on again?

Or will moments turn into feathers to tickle
Faces,
Palms,
Feet,
As we relax to meet our lovers?

Will the earth flower there,
Produce immortal fruits to keep us alive?

All that might happen when we die.
But why wait?
Do it all now,
Do it today.

An explanation of love

On a peak in the Atlas Mountains
There is a moon.
Three are stars tattooed to its heel.

The stream nearby
Flows to the right.

There are pine trees, a sea of them.
It's too dark to see them,
But you can still feel them.

This is love.

Dream

You are in a beautiful place.
        Dusk strikes.
Grass quakes beneath your feet.

In the distance a gazelle gazes.
Trees roar with winds.
Branches clap and leaves swing
Right,
Left
And centre
To embrace the muddy soil.

The dark mountain has a snowy peak,
As if a bottle of milk was spilt on a black table.

Everything in this vision must stay this way.

The phone rings.
The dream ends.

Never mind,
Tonight you will fall asleep again and go back there.

Yellow Flower

Deep yellow colour,
Spots of green.

On the side,
The petals are sharp as a butcher's knife.

The crown misses some parts.

The short stamen,
Moves in a zigzag
To reach the bud,
Wait for rain,
Suck it
And grow old.

Beautiful thought

Beautiful thought
Where are you?

Come to me

Leave the world,
Roll on its palm
And ooze into my head.

Come on in
I beg you to start roaming my brain
Alley by alley.

In the middle whirl
Whirl and whirl
Like a Dervish whirl

Leave your fragrance
In each nerve
Put me into a trance
Sedate me with the beautiful.

This body

This body is like an Arabian oasis,
From a distance it looks plentiful,
Shiny,
Bright,
Full of obedient water.

You lower your head to drink

A wavy reflection appears in the water,
You calmly watch it float away.

A friendship

Born prematurely,
It reaches maturity in just a few hours.

Now in a nursing home,
It enjoys the view from a top floor window onto the canals outside.

The water thickens,
Eventually
It becomes a solid earth.

The friendship loses shape
And is now empty, like the vase on the window sill
Where it has been standing for the last seventeen hours.

Outside,
There is a queue of roses at the door
Millions of them.

It takes everyone by surprise,
And jumps into the canal.

Cemetery flowers

Near the exit,
They lean towards passers-by and whisper,
'See you later as a visitor or a resident.
Either way,
See you later'.

Stand up and walk

Stand up and walk.
Breathe in and hold your breath,
Keep your head up,
Place two hands on the floor
And push your body into a standing position.
Wipe your feet clean
Watch out for dust between the toes,
Then breathe out and walk.
Do it now
      Please
Stand up and walk.

Acknowledgments

Thanks must go to Middlesbrough artist and poet, Margaret Williams, for her help in editing this collection, and for the image on the front-cover. Thanks also to Bob Beagrie and Andy Willoughby at Teesside University. I am grateful to the editors of the following publications where some of these poems first appeared – *Black Light Engine Room*, *Break-Out*, *Ofipress* (Mexico), *Parnasso* (Finland) and *Palestine Chronicles* (USA).

Notes

Sorry
Shawarma are thinly sliced meats, usually lamb or chicken, wrapped in pita bread.

I feel I should speak of the city
Assalamu Alaikum is the Islamic greeting 'Peace be upon you'. A *kanafeh* is a cheese-pastry soaked in sweet sugar-based syrup. A *kobbah* is a raditional Aleppo dish of wheat, meat and nuts. حلو يا رايح وين is an expression often used by Aleppo taxi-drivers to catch customers. A *yashmak* is a veil worn by Muslim women to cover their faces in public.

We have just arrived at the entrance of Arabia
Habiby is the Arabic word for lover.

It's all about love
A *misbaḥah* is a string of prayer beads, like the Catholic rosary, which is often used by Muslims to keep track of counting in *tasbih*. A *hammam* is the Arabian version of the Turkish communal bath. *Barkouk* is the Arabic word for a prune.

This is Amsterdam
Wok to Walk is the name of a takeaway in Amsterdam. Zaan's cafe is in Zaan, a small town near Amsterdam.

A visit to Rio's Parque Lage
Parque Lage is a public park in the city of Rio de Janeiro, located in the Jardim Botânico neighbourhood at the foot of the Corcovado.

What if
Christ the Redeemer is an Art Deco statue of Jesus Christ in Rio de Janeiro, Brazil, created by French sculptor Paul Landowski and built by the engineer Heitor da Silva Costa Brazil in collaboration with the French engineer Albert Caquot.

To write for and to Morocco

Jemma is the Arabic word for Friday. *Jinnah* is the Arabic word for Paradise. The Al Bahia palace is in Marrakech. Built in the nineteenth-century, it reflects both Moroccan and Islamic styles of architecture.